W9-AGG-273
DREAM
FREE PIZZA!!
FREE THE LEASH KIDS!
DOWN WITH PANTSING
POWER TO THE ELECTRONICS!
UNDER BITES UNITE!!
RELIGIOUS FREEDOM FOR HOLY COWS!
YES WE TAN!
SHARKS
H8
MEALS ON WHEELS ON THE BUS
MATH COUNTS
HUGS NOT SLUGS
I LIKE BIKE
LEGALIZE CANDY FOR BREAKFAST

A DEFINITION OF " ACTIVISM " :

ACTIVISM IS NOT JUST A HOBBY OR JOB...
NOT JUST FOR THE HIPPIES,
OR THE LARGE ANGRY MOB.
THIS WORD IS AN ACTION
WITH THINGS TO ACHIEVE -
WHICH IS MOSTLY:
TO STAND UP FOR WHAT YOU BELIEVE.
AND IT CAN START ANYWHERE. ANYTIME.
EVEN, RIGHT THIS SECOND -
IF YOU MADE UP YOUR MIND.
AS YOU FLIP THE NEXT PAGES,
WHY NOT THINK ABOUT HOW
YOU CAN DO YOUR OWN PART,
AND YOUR PART CAN START... NOW!

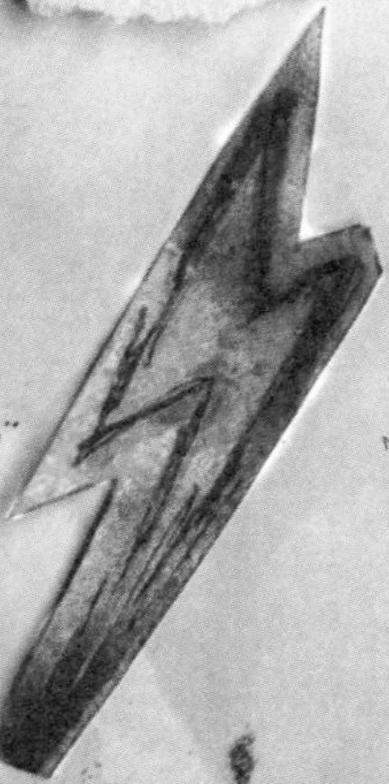

ATTN: A LITTLE RADICAL / PRETTYPLEASE
2240 ENCINITAS BLVD., SUITE D #194
ENCINITAS, CA. 92024

RESPONSIBLY PRINTED IN KOREA
1ST EDITION PRINT 2017
NOINVITATION.COM

A LITTLE
RADICAL
BY
DANICA & JASON
RUSSELL

THIS BOOK
BELONGS
TO:

ALL FOR:
GAVIN
AND
EVERLEY
WE ARE DOING OUR BEST, AS PARENTS, TO GIVE YOU THE WORLD, and WE ARE DOING OUR BEST AS PEOPLE TO MAKE THAT WORLD SOMETHING WORTH HAVING.
MIND, HEART, LIPS.
- MUM + DAD

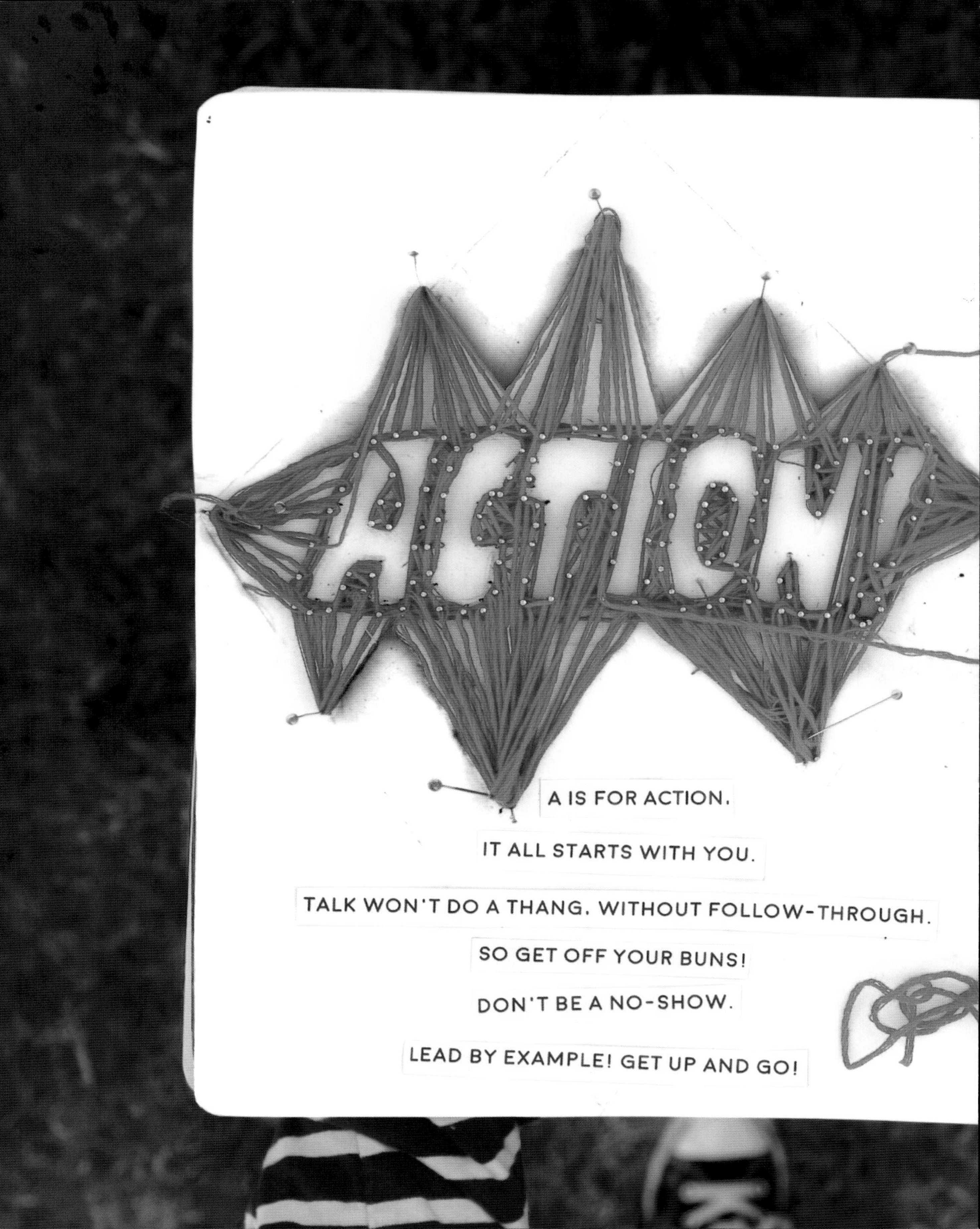

ACTION!

A IS FOR ACTION.

IT ALL STARTS WITH YOU.

TALK WON'T DO A THANG, WITHOUT FOLLOW-THROUGH.

SO GET OFF YOUR BUNS!

DON'T BE A NO-SHOW.

LEAD BY EXAMPLE! GET UP AND GO!

NOTHING WILL CHANGE IF YOU JUST STAND STILL.
COME ALIVE! TAKE ACTION!
YOU CAN, IF YOU WILL.

B IS FOR BOYCOTT, AND WHEN TO SAY "NO."
SWIM UPSTREAM! DON'T JUST "GO WITH THE FLOW."

IF IT'S BAD, DON'T BUY IT. PULL A SWITCHAROO.

WHEN YOU TAKE A STAND, AND DO A DON'T- DO.

SOMETIMES A "MUST" BECOMES A MUST NOT.

BAN, BLOCK, BARRICADE, AND BEGIN A BOYCOTT.

C IS CREATE: ALL THAT'S YET TO BE.
MAKE SOMETHING NEW. SET YOUR DREAMS FREE.
MUSIC AND DANCE. FILM AND DESIGN -
CAN MAKE US FEEL FEELINGS.
AND CHANGE MANY MINDS.

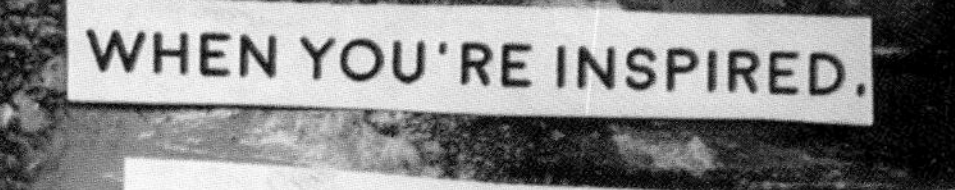
WHEN YOU'RE INSPIRED,
MAKE SOMETHING GREAT.
WE COLOR THE WORLD,
EVERY TIME WE CREATE!

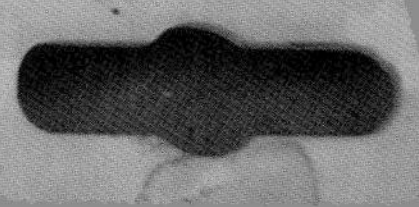

Defend.

D IS FOR DEFEND! BEING BOLD. TAKING AIM.

PICK UP YOUR SHIELD AND GET IN THE GAME.

PROTECT YOUR BELIEFS. LIVE LIFE WITHOUT FEAR!

STAY SHARP AND FIGHT SMART. BE THE TIP OF THE SPEAR.

ACTIVISTS MUST BE AS BRAVE AS A KNIGHT.

STAND UP. AND STAND STRONG.

TO DEFEND WHAT IS RIGHT.

EXPLO
Containing the Greatest Amount of Land.
HEMISPHERE
THE LETTER E IS FOR EXPLORE.
AND WHERE YOU'VE NEVER GONE BEFORE.
WHEN YOU TRAVEL NEW PLACES, AND MAKE A NEW FRIEND,
YOUR FEARS BECOME SMALLER AND DIFFERENCES END.
MOUNTAINS IN EASTERN HEMISPHER
EUROPE.
ASIA, AFRICA & AUSTRA
WRANGEL I.
Melville Sound
RICA
WOR

ADVENTURE IS WAITING OUTSIDE YOUR FRONT DOOR!
GO WANDER AND WONDER. EXPAND AND EXPLORE!

F IS FOR FAIL. WHICH MEANS: TO NOT-WIN.
YOU LIVE AND YOU LEARN. GET UP! TRY AGAIN.
FACE ALL YOUR MONSTERS!
DON'T RUN AND HIDE.
YOU CAN STAY ON YOUR BOTTOM,
OR FIND THE UPSIDE.

JUST- DO. NOT. GIVE UP!

START FRESH. THINK IT OUT.

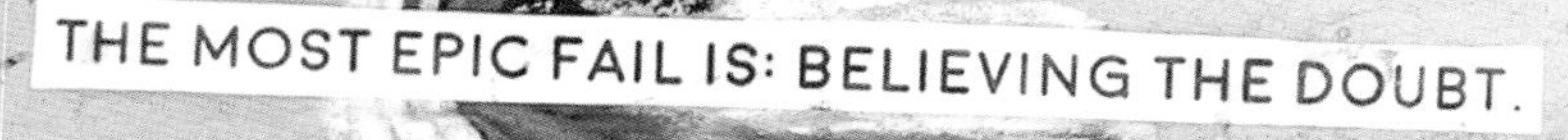

THE MOST EPIC FAIL IS: BELIEVING THE DOUBT.

FAIL.

GIVE
IN GOD WE TRUST

G IS FOR GIVE. ALL THE THINGS WE CAN DO.

YOUR TIME AND YOUR TALENT
ARE TREASURES TOO.

IT'S NOT JUST ABOUT WHAT YOU HAVE IN THE BANK:
HOW YOU'LL BE PRAISED, OR HOW YOU'LL BE THANKED.

'CUZ THE MOST "WELL-OFF" PEOPLE
ARE THOSE WHO LIVE
WITH THEIR ARMS AND HEARTS OPEN,
READY TO GIVE.

HEART

H IS FOR HEART, AND WHAT PUMPS YOU UP:
YOUR PASSION, YOUR PURPOSE,
AND WHAT FILLS YOUR CUP.

AN ALARM CLOCK INSIDE,
GETTING YOU OUT OF BED.

IT KEEPS YOU AWAKE,
FROM YOUR TOES TO YOUR HEAD.

IF IT'S IN YOUR BLOOD,
IT WILL REACH EVERY PART.

ACTS OF LOVE OVERFLOW
WHEN YOU WORK FROM THE HEART.

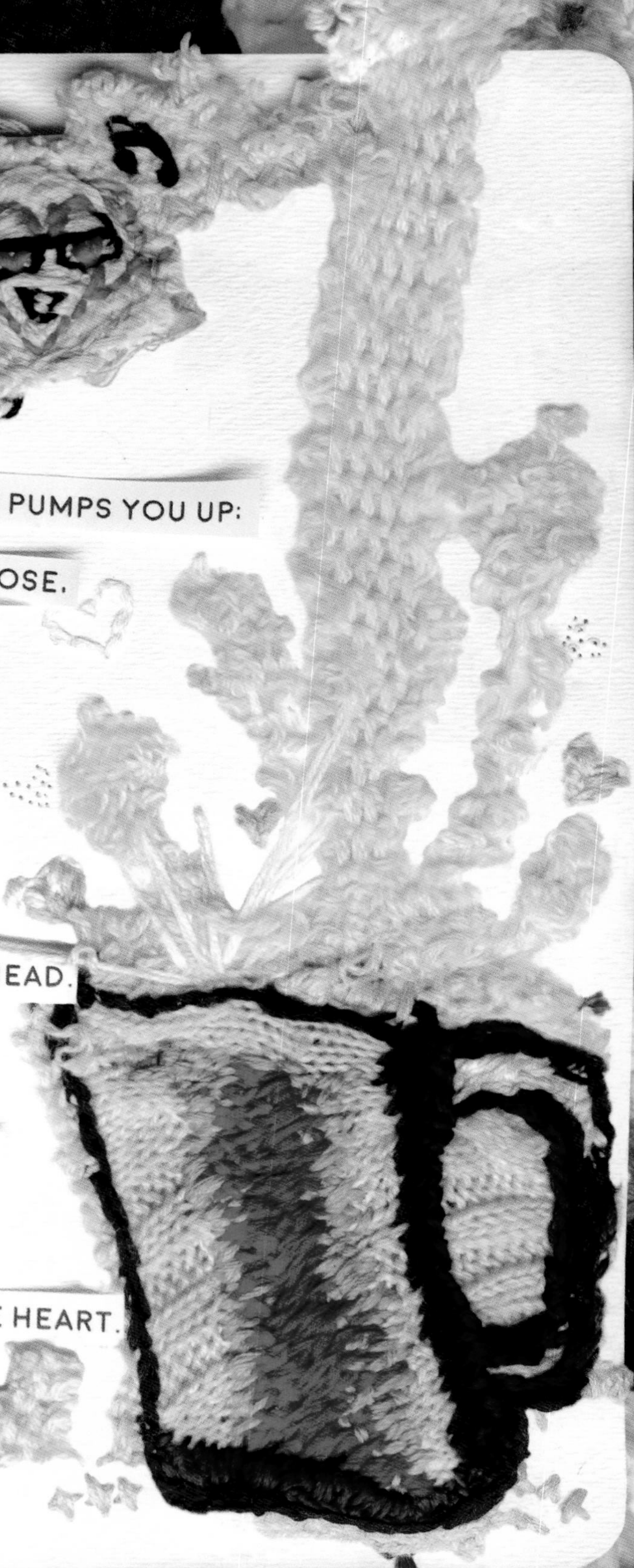

I IS FOR IMPACT. AND WHAT YOU INTEND.
WHAT IS THE TARGET? HOW DOES IT END?
IMPACT

IT'S HAVING A GOAL AND CLIMBING THE CHART.
HOW FAR HAVE YOU COME
SINCE YOU MADE YOUR START?
YOU CAUSE AN EFFECT. IT'S A MATTER OF FACT.
ANYTIME YOU TAKE ACTION,
YOU MAKE AN IMPACT.

J IS FOR JUSTICE.
WHICH MEANS: WHAT IS RIGHT.
THOUGH. GOOD VS. EVIL
IS NOT BLACK AND WHITE.
IT SHOULDN'T COME DOWN
TO WHERE YOU WERE BORN.
PEOPLE ARE EQUALS.
BUT THE WORLD IS STILL TORN.
IF SOMETHING'S NOT FAIR,
OR DOES NOT SEEM DESERVED.
SPEAK UP. TIP THE SCALES.
SEE THAT JUSTICE IS SERVED.

HANCOC
be sure

Kindness

K IS FOR KINDNESS:
THE WAY WE SHOULD ACT:
BEING THE PERSON YOU HOPE TO ATTRACT.
DON'T BE A BULLY, AND DO NOT BE CRUEL.
WE TREAD THE SAME WATER, DON'T PEE IN THE POOL!
"DIFFERENT" AIN'T WRONG, SO OPEN YOUR MIND!
YOU DO YOU, LET THEM TOO, BUT WE ALL MUST BE KIND!

L IS FOR LISTEN. THE BEST WAY TO LEARN.
DON'T NOD AND FAKE IT. 'TILL YOUR TALKING TURN.
YOU WANT TO HELP OTHERS? THEY KNOW WHAT THEY NEED.
THINK WITH THEM. NOT FOR THEM.
DON'T LEAD A STAMPEDE.
YOU CAN'T KNOW-IT-ALL
WITH JUST ONE POINT OF VIEW.
LISTEN.
AND RE-THINK
WHAT YOU THOUGHT YOU KNEW.
AH HA!

LISTEN
IF YOU DIDN'T HEAR,
LET ME SAY IT AGAIN...
TO TEACH YOU MUST LEARN
AND TO LEARN: JUST LISTEN!
ZIP

MARC

M IS FOR MARCH... I DARE YOU TO MOVE.

BEAT ON YOUR DRUM, AND GET IN THE GROOVE.

POSTING A PIC, OR A LINK, OR A 'LIKE'

IS A DIGITAL MOVEMENT, BUT DON'T DROP THE MIC.

LET'S ALL JOIN THE BAND!

LET'S RALLY AND CHEER!

IT'S YOUR MOVE TO MAKE...

MARCHING ORDERS ARE HERE.

N IS FOR NOW.

WHERE YOU ARE.

WHERE YOU START.

THERE'S NO INVITATION

FOR YOU TO TAKE PART.

EVERY IDEA.

AND GREAT NEW BREAKTHROUGH

WAS MADE UP BY SOMEONE

NO SMARTER THAN YOU.

OPEN THE PRESENT.

WHO KNOWS WHAT WILL LAST?

WRITE THE FUTURE RIGHT NOW.

BEFORE IT'S THE PAST.

YOU
ARE
HERE.

O IS ORGANIC.

QUITE NATURALLY.

ALL LIVING THINGS.
FROM THE SKY TO THE SEA.

REDUCE AND RECYCLE AND ALSO REUSE.

TO KEEP OUR GREENS GREEN.

AND CLEAR UP OUR BLUES.

ORGANIC
SO, EAT YOUR GRANOLA!
LET CHICKENS ROAM FREE!
WE'LL LIVE LONGER LIVES.
ORGANIC-LY!

P IS FOR PEACE.
FOR THE WORLD AND YOUR SOUL.
TO LIVE WITHOUT WAR
IS THE ULTIMATE GOAL.
THERE IS A PLACE WE ALL LIKE TO PICTURE:
NO BORDERS.
OR HOARDERS.
OR TWISTED UP SCRIPTURE.
IT'S NOT JUST A HIPPIE'S
SONG AND DANCE.
ALL WE ARE SAYING IS:
GIVE PEACE A CHANCE.

QUALIT

Q IS FOR QUALITY.
WORK DONE WELL.
BE SHARP AS A DIAMOND.
AND CLEAR AS A BELL.
THERE ARE SO MANY CAUSES.
IGNORED OR NEGLECTED.
POLISH. ASTONISH.
DO MORE THAN EXPECTED.
BRING YOUR BEST.
AND BEST YOU WILL BE.
THE HIGHER THE STANDARDS.
THE MORE QUALITY.

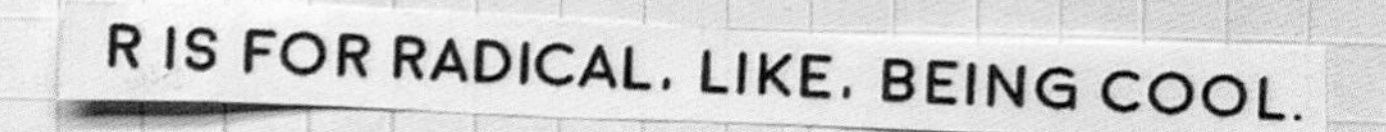
R IS FOR RADICAL. LIKE. BEING COOL.

QUESTIONING EVERYTHING. BREAKING THE RULE.

SHAKING THINGS UP LEADS TO NEW SOLUTIONS.

YOU NEED SOME CRAZY TO START REVOLUTIONS!

RADICALS ARE RAD AND PURSUE WHAT IS TRUE.

BEING BORING'S A SIN.

WHAT'S RAD ABOUT YOU?

RADICAL

S IS FOR SPARK. THE START OF A FIRE.
HOW ONE LITTLE LIFE CAN IGNITE AND INSPIRE.
STRIKE WHEN YOU'RE HOT. EVEN IF YOU BURN OUT.
YOU MAY NEVER KNOW WHAT YOUR GLOW BRINGS ABOUT.
MOST PEOPLE ARE AFRAID OF THE DARK.
FOR THE WORLD TO LIGHT UP. WE JUST NEED YOUR SPARK.

T IS FOR TRIBE.
YOU ARE NOT ALONE!
LET YOUR GOALS AND YOUR WORRIES
BE SHARED AND MADE KNOWN.
THEY BELIEVED IN YOU FIRST,
AND HELP YOU GALORE.
A LITTLE MARSHMALLOW
CAN BE SO MUCH S'MORE!
YOU MAY NEED A NUDGE,
OR JUST A HIGH FIVE.
WHEN YOU SET UP CAMP,
FIND YOUR TRIBE TO SURVIVE.

TRIBE

U MEANS UNITE. BEING PART OF THE WHOLE.
ORGANIZED. SYNCHRONIZED. FOR THE SAME GOAL.
ONE HUNDRED HEADS ARE *BETTER* THAN ONE.
JOINING TOGETHER. TO GET THE JOB DONE.
IF YOU WANT TO MOVE FAST.
GO ALONE TOWARD THE FIGHT.
IF YOU WANT TO GO FAR.
ALL THE TRIBES MUST UNITE!

V IS FOR VISION.
THE DREAMS WE CAN DREAM
SAIL OFF THE WORLD'S EDGE.
RIP OPEN THE SEAM.
SEE. KNOWLEDGE IS KNOWING
WHAT'S ALREADY THERE.
BUT IMAGINE WHAT'S NOT!
PULL IT OUT OF THIN AIR!
BE WILD. INVENTIVE.
LOOK DEEP WITHIN.
THEN. SET YOUR SIGHTS HIGH.
TO SEE THE VISION!

VISION
8
5
2

PRO
CON
No.
TOTAL PRO:
Conclusion:
Plan of Action:
esc
F1
F2
F3
F4
F5
F6
F7
F8
F9

WORK WILL REQUIRE A DOUBLE YOU,

TO STAY ON THE JOB, TILL YOUR FACE IS BLUE.

STAY UP LATE, AND PUSH THROUGH THE PAIN.

NOTHING THAT'S GREAT WAS EASILY GAINED.

IT'S MORE THAN A BURST, OR A QUICK KNEE JERK:

NOTHING GETS DONE, IF YOU DON'T GET TO WORK!

X IS FOR ZEE-ROG-RA-FEE.

PASSING IDEAS, BETWEEN YOU AND ME.

PRINT POSTERS, AND FLIERS, BE SEEN AND HEARD.
YOU CAN SAY A LOT WITHOUT SAYING A WORD.
HAND OUT YOUR MESSAGE, SO OTHERS RELATE -
AND YOU'LL BE A XEROX
OF THOSE WHO WERE GREAT!

IF YOU KNOW WHO YOU ARE,
AND YOU KNOW WHERE YOU STAND,
THEN, WHATEVER YOU DO,
IS BOUND TO BE GRAND.
BE HOPEFUL. BE HELPFUL.
LOVE IS IN THE DETAILS.
BE YOU IN THE SLUMS,
AND BE YOU IN TUX TAILS.
'CUZ IT ONLY TAKES ONE TO STAND UP AND SAY
"ENOUGH IS ENOUGH, AND TODAY IS THE DAY."
IF YOU WANT SOMETHING CHANGED,
AND WISH THINGS WERE MADE NEW...
MAYBE,
WE'VE ALL JUST BEEN WAITING FOR
YOU.

YOU.

h I t

ive [illegible] e is [illegible] lips fosing [illegible] ry

t m [illegible] sk [illegible] a kin [illegible] ne

ha [illegible] ct d' l

t [illegible] veliat

[illegible] be.

n.

[illegible] ke

[illegible] or [illegible] te

[illegible] capt

[illegible] e g

Volh [illegible] the

S in me [illegible] eamedo

[illegible] e re [illegible] a [illegible] l is agre

[illegible] ing [illegible] gerty. Tur

ZZZ...ZZZ...ZZZ...ZZZ...ZZZ...ZZZ

ZZZ...ZZZ...ZZZ...ZZZ...ZZZ

ZZZ...ZZZ...ZZZ...ZZZ...ZZZ...ZZZ

...ZZZ...ZZZ...ZZZ...ZZZ...ZZZ...ZZZ

Z...ZZZ

AT THE END OF IT ALL.
GET AFTER THE ZZZZZZZ'S.
YOU WILL GO BAD.
IF YOU DON'T DEEP FREEZE.
YOU MAY WANT TO WORK
TILL YOU MELT LIKE ICE CREAM
BUT IF YOU DON'T SLEEP.
THEN HOW CAN YOU DREAM?
GIVE IT A REST!
THERE ARE MORE DAYS TO SEIZE!
ACTIVISTS ARE HEROES.
WHO NEED SUPERSIZED ZZZZZZZ'S.

WITH YOUR PAINT! COLOR! GLITTER! STICKERS!
CUT OUT, DECORATE, & SEND THIS LOVE LETTER BACK TO US
& YOU'LL GET:

1. AN EMAILED DISCOUNT CODE SO THAT YOU CAN SEND A BOOK TO A FRIEND!

2. THE CHANCE TO BE POSTED ON OUR SOCIAL MEDIA ALONGSIDE LITTLE RADICALS FROM AROUND THE WORLD!

FOLLOW US@ ALITTLERADICAL.COM
WWW.FACEBOOK.COM/ALITTLE RADICAL

GLUE GLUE GLUE

FOLD FOLD

(YOUR PICTURE GOES HERE!)

MY NAME IS

BUT YOU CAN CALL ME

I AM __ YEARS OLD +I LIVE IN

MY FAVORITE LETTER IS

BECAUSE

FOLD FOLD

I AM A LITTLE RADICAL BECAUSE I MAKE THE WORLD BETTER BY

PS.

MY EMAIL IS:

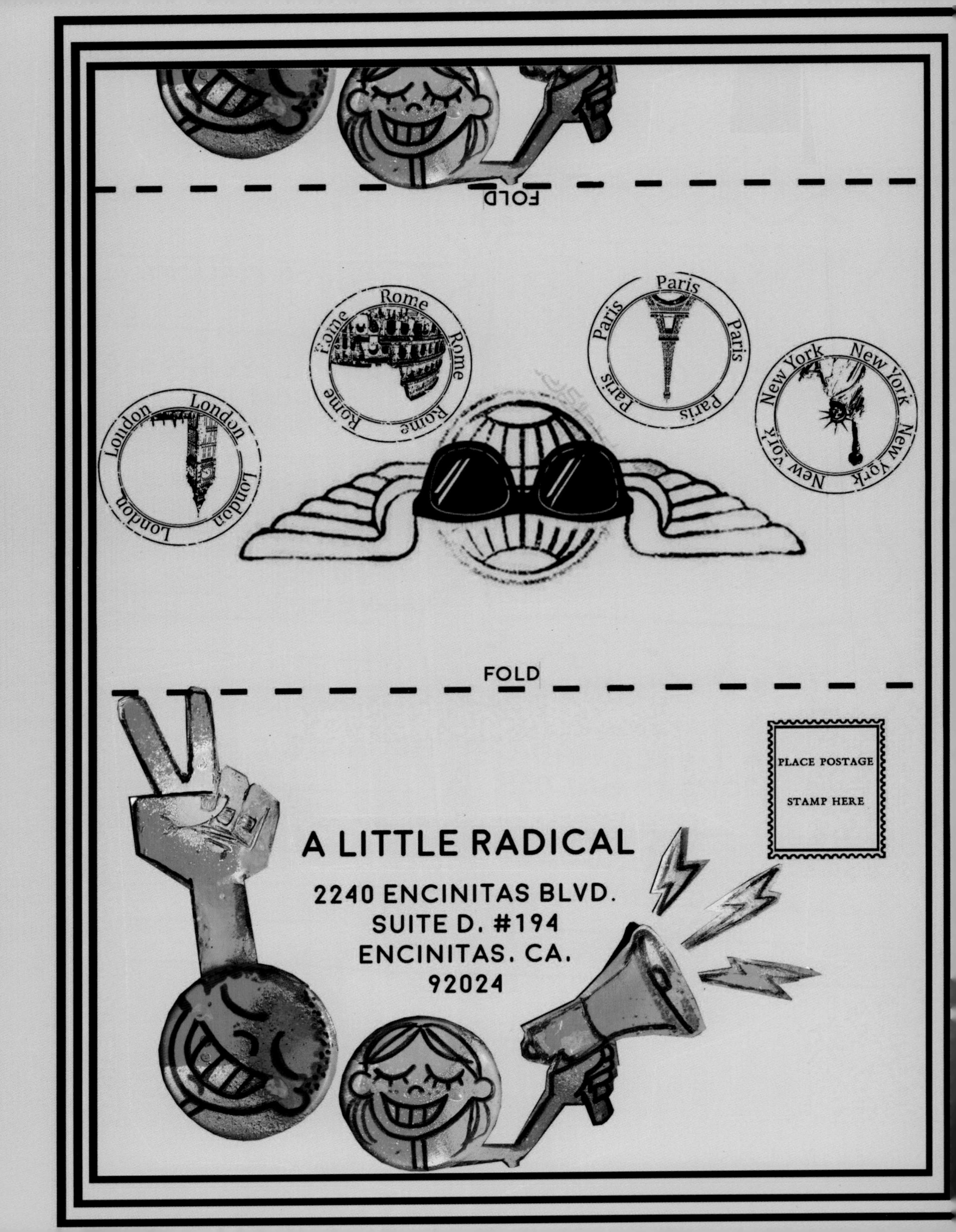
FOLD
Rome
Paris
London
New York
FOLD
PLACE POSTAGE
STAMP HERE
A LITTLE RADICAL
2240 ENCINITAS BLVD.
SUITE D. #194
ENCINITAS. CA.
92024

TURN ME INTO
A STENCIL!

TURN ME INTO
A STENCIL!

SPECIAL THANKS
KATIE MICHELLE THOMPSON
ANNIKA LANGE
BABY BREEDEN
CHARLIE & PENNY FLOETER
JACK DANIEL & ARABELLA
THE RYNESS FAMILY
ACE CURTIS, GOLDIE DANIELSON, CASH ELIASON, DECLAN ROACH, & HANNA JERMASEK
FOSTER MARSHMAN
CAROL ANN HUNTER
JOHN & ROBYN DOWNING
KARYN OVERSTREET HEALY
HENDRIX & HARPER HANSEN
ELENI GIANULIS
JOSH & BIT
JOHN & RAE SPRUILL
CAMERON BROWN
JOLIE & JACK GASTINEAU
CHRISTIAN & ISLA PIERCE
ILY, WALKER, MASON, JACKSON, PARK
MORGAN KITSY AIDEN NIPPER
TAHNEE YOON
JUSTIN, KIRA, KOHL, EVERETT, EMERY & GREYSON WHEELER
ANGELA & JORDAN BENTLEY & JANE DIANGE
KIMBERLY ORIAS
AUDREY & LIBERTY
MOUNTAIN VIEW HIGH SCHOOL INVISIBLE CHILDREN CLUB
KEVIN TROUT
NOAH, ROSALYN, JONAH, THEODORE & LEVI.
CASH & FINLEY KELLEY
EILEY JOY BOHLINGER
ALISON TRELEAVEN
SEAN DAVID CARASS
THE HANCOCK FAMILY
CONNOR HUGHES
LIAM & FINLEY RYAN
OWEN SPRUILL
AMY LOUISE COLLINS
HUDSON & BENNETT NUTTER
DJ, SHANNA, ADLER, SEGAN & PENN VIOLA

PARKER & LEAH SILLIMAN
KATIE BRADEL
GUY RAZ
DAWSON MARTIN
CARSON, CASSIDY, & CADE SMITH
XANTHOS FAMILY
NEIL, RACHEL, GRIFFIN & GEMMA BLUMENTHAL
ASHLEY D'AGOSTINI
GEORGIA ROWEN WOODS
ERIN MADIERA
JJ & HANNALEE + CLOUD
LENNON WINTER LEWIS
AUTUMN & AVERY ERMANIS
MEG GARDNER SKINNER
LAURIE BETH DIMAGGIO
HAROON & TASNEEM ASKARI
STEVE WITMER
KINLEY MERAE COX
PAUL & SHERYL RUSSELL
JESSE KLEKAMP
EVANGELINE & MERIDON WILK
COWABUNGA CHILDCARE
JEFF&EMILY FULKERSON
JENNY BATES
ELLIE PLUMMER
NAVMIT DHESI
GREG & JOLYNN BROWN
MARK FOIS & FAMILY
LAUREN EDWARDS
JOURNEY PARTON
HIEU HO
MADDIE MEEKS
LISA &WADE
NATALIE WARNE
PHOEBE, GUS, RUBY & ISLA DUTHIE
HANNAH SHANE REDFORD-SHUMATE
REED WILLIAM GUTZWILLER
THE STEVERS FAMILY
JAY SALBERT
MELISSA PATERAS
SANDY
TRENNON, NOAH, LYLA, & TATE MCNAUGHTON
OTTO & MAGS THOMSON
DON & CATHY SLEEPER
STEPHEN & BEKS OPPERMAN
RENEE, CURTIS, SAILOR, & RIVER KAUFFMAN